When the Sun Turns Green

When the Sun Turns Green

JANE McKIE

First published in Great Britain in 2009 by
Polygon, an imprint of Birlinn Ltd

West Newington House
10 Newington Road
Edinburgh
EH9 1QS

www.birlinn.co.uk

ISBN 978 184697 134 1

British Library Cataloguing-in-Publication Data
A catalogue record for this book is available on
request from the British Library.

Typeset in Great Britain by Antony Gray
Printed and bound by CPI Antony Rowe, Chippenham

for Vee Vee and Theo

Contents

Acknowledgements

Some poems from this collection have appeared in the following publications: *Island Magazine, Other Poetry, Pennine Platform,* Granta Books' *New Writing, The Shantytown Anomaly, V: New International Writing from Edinburgh, One Magazine, The Frogmore Papers, Smiths Knoll* and *Envoi.* Warm thanks to Sarah Ream for her perceptive comments and unflagging attention to poetic detail, and to Phil Raines for being a very patient non-poetry-writing reader.

The Perception of Whiteness

It's how the eye sees green stars:
always white. Never emerald, olive,
moss. Transparency underpins sight,

the ribs of the Pantone fan
fold into light like milk, flour, butter
to temper earth's colours.

She was a mistake.

In a parallel universe,
he shouts out for viridian,
shamrock, chartreuse – vivid

alternatives to monochrome.
There, every fleck in her father's iris
is a proto-star.

Cloud Family

The sky is a slow caravan,
embryo clouds
forming fingers, hands
to span any gaps.
Sister, I would reach out to you,
coach you in how to keep
a body on the brink of dissolution.

Brother, I can't save you –
you've given up your grip,
white noise replacing
our sibling tongues.

Connective tissue
is severed
to the sound of the stars.

Mother, Father,
you too have changed
as I change.

The only thing that keeps us kin
is the infant inside us all, helix

endlessly unfolding –

Order of Birth

First

They bow down as she passes
like the sea does – wild flowers and sedges
tall as children, their hair green and gold;
they are python-headed, top-heavy with seeds.
Mother of grasses, mother of slender ghosts,
Luna's face is clay-white, her expression remote.

They all want to dance with the small goddess
playing beside the canal. No taller than a child,
she looks human in moonlight. She is too close
to the water's edge, too far from the tow-path.
I lift her out of the reeds and carry her home,
lightest void, to my own maternal bed.

Second

Luna, the first one,
pulled her red brother from the womb
not worried about blood on her christening dress.

I watch her hands, small white instruments,
cupped around his crown. She is luminous,
but now I have a new light in the sky to navigate by,

a second – solar – child to tend.
Luna dances at the birth, strong girl, too soon
to tell if she will love her brother more, or less, than me.

Grandmother Ikons

Grandmother in Silver

She is a teapot, all those trinkets
that she couldn't bear to use or sell,
rings garnering dust on the shelf,
or in the musty nests of drawers lined
with triple-boiled handkerchiefs.
She said they were silver,
but they could have been tin.
In my youth, it was the same thing:
a glint like the ribs of the sea glistening
with moonshine; her hand on my arm
telling me stories, truths and untruths.

Grandmother in Pearl

Her off-white soft slip, stored since the fifties,
lace on top of expensive silk, scared me.
It wasn't her, that folded lozenge
at the back of the closet, loose, shot through
with light – the lustre of painted nails,
worked ivory embedded in wood.
To me, she was thick brown nylon,
tweedy coats for the garden
bloating out a spindle frame.
No indulgence. Little adornment.
Always digging, always the same.

Grandmother in Lapis

I almost forgot: there was one brooch
she sometimes wore – blue, bird's-egg blue,
rusty nail of a pin harpooning her loopy cardigan.
She could be sharp as an ibis,
no blunt edges, getting to the eye of a wound
with barbed words as though spearing
fish for supper. It was how she survived:
eating little, sleeping less, watching
for gaps between the clouds
where the sky was like lapis lazuli.

Grandmother in Gold

I remember her panning the earth
for its riches, sifting ordinary seeds
from nuggets of gold. This metal
could germinate: miraculous plants, diminutive
as tortoiseshell wallflowers, their pollen
gold dust. In the end, her many ailments
meant nothing beside her hunger for Midas;
the final ague was just her bones
growing up towards the orb of the sun.

The Ascension of Nana

You flit across my sightline seemingly untethered,
looser than you were in life, more mischievous.
Gathered up in your best dress like a Fabergé egg,
you tickle the earth with ectoplasmic feathers.

We had always speculated that your blood was blue.
Can it be true when you died you became a tsarina?
You were the pole star, fixed point, firmest rudder;
when your mind clamped down, no-one could budge you.

Grandmother, this new frivolity is ravishingly weightless –
gowned in picture-book clouds, you have finally taken off.

Hawthorn Queen

It was one of those last swarms,
a blood-red immolation of ladybirds
so thick
the air appeared pixellated.

Traffic stopped.

My mother grasped my hand, and together
we picked a path across hot tarmac
decorated with appliqué wing-cases.
They buckled like molten plastic, stuck
to the bottom of our sandals –
mottled chitin, black gravel.

I looked up and saw tears on my mother's chin.

Quaking, she led me past the stationary cars,
their engines overheated. All the time
more dazed ladybirds
gathered in her golden hair
as if she guaranteed safe passage
or could halt the insect blizzard.

Looking up, I saw a Hawthorn Queen,
her crown alive with crawling berries.

Only Child

One two
Touch the red wall

Three four
Smell the red rose

Five six
Salute the red sun

Seven eight
Mum's safe again

Nine ten
She'll be home at day's end

Clocks

The sun breaks trunks
into staved shadows.

One spear-tip creeps up
on your makeshift fort
like a long clock-hand.

Soon time to go in, Jonathan,
your mother is calling.

You shot me earlier,
but I don't mind. I giggled.
Your arrow, my heart

all over my ruled exercise book:
J loves J forever, 1975.

Bouillabaisse

She had always marvelled
at the birthing of fishes,
the bob of jellied eggs
double-bagged in fluid
glinting like opals.

She would run her fingers near them,
feel their gibbous drift
against the skin of her tips,
careful not to dislodge them,
to unstick the bunch.

Later, she would be more fearless
and net them up, pallid, drizzling
out of the mesh, festooned in green weed.

But her very finest discoveries
were those first tentative dips
into a curiously refracted world
where eggs would blink like crocodile eyes,
the life inside
tiny black pupils struggling to dilate.

The Assignation

We are the voyeurs
in the thicket, hoping for titillation,
surprised by our shame.

New grass, white-green shoots,
crushed. At first we laugh –
she is our sister

brought here by her silly wish
to impress the gang:
I am more worldly;

I am not just a figment,
a slip. Her mane hangs down
like a bang, crowned head

bridling at the handling
despite herself. And we wonder
suddenly why we are here

at this most private of acts –
maidens wooing, unicorn
trapped. Our blushes

rise like tree sap
and I imagine myself buried
under the leaf mound,

lost to humiliation.
Is this what we can all expect?
No ceremony, a quick undoing.

Playing on the Groynes

There is a Morse code, dashes and dots,
that has been forgotten. It punctuates
the south coast at intervals,

stout wooden fences to pleat
the sand into apportioned pastures –
common land, imperfectly divided.

Those groynes were diving boards, walls
between a tranche of castles, each leaning
into the greater subsidence of the sea;

they were gymnasts' bars between the far horizon
and firmer land, one that we all walked
with crazy surety. If we slipped, it was only a few feet

to a bed of stones. Alone, we would never
be so brave, took it step by slow step,
a gnomic voice sounding in our minds:

tread carefully, child, along the ranks of groynes,
they are less loving than you think – possible pitfall,
another of those dangerous thin lines.

The Rose Wall

That red rose wall where my knuckles were grazed –
my first bike veering to the side – felt like brambles
but was brick, the brick of all the houses, all the gardens
bristling in our neighbourhood. I was never any good
at telling them apart – the houses, the gardens,
the grid of days that kept each plot separate from the next.

The whole of early memory is laced with sameness:
same summers, same toys, same circumstantial friends.
I miss that magic, binding me in place. Is that red wall
still standing, rose-faced, shy of the wider world?

Here Be Monsters

They parade across the parchment map
with their dragon's breath, their sealing wax,
a string of them: some with spliced tails;
others with two legs, a human heart
and easily wounded pride.

Like them, I am a drawing of Indian ink,
sinking myself into stories, never coming up
for air. Once upon a time,

in Cornwall, I saw my first half-man
hiding in the garden. Since then, they rarely
reveal themselves, but I know they are there –
there in the grotesques wrought by myth,
there in my mother's dryad voice

following the course of St Nectan's Glen.
Sometimes I hear them calling, *Come, come away*
to the west, come back to the red river you were born in.

Knucker

The sky reflected in the Knucker's pool –
iridescent like lighter fuel, optical illusion

of petrol and touch-paper poised to ignite.
I was twelve when I heard it was bottomless

or – another theory – it met with the sea,
underground caves housing a serpentine beast:

the Lyminster Knucker. I should have loved
the vanquishing boy, local lad, Jim Pulk;

I should have longed to kiss his forehead
daubed with blood, congratulate his audacity.

Instead, at night, the monster swam to me
in practiced spirals, murmuring my name.

I was too young for serenades, too young to see
the ancient wyrm claim my flooded chambers.

Snakebite

I stepped on a snake
and it stung me in the softest place –
the foot's arch where flesh is pale
for it never sees the light of day.

If it had been the heel,
perhaps I would have survived that bite
sharp as a fork's tine, but small,
so small it didn't seem significant.

New-moon snake, you are in orbit,
a streak of half-light that never quite
illuminates the ground. My foot found you
and you found my weakest spot

in retaliation. I don't blame you though.
That poison you sent straight to my heart
was quick and sweet. If I had been shod in iron,
I wouldn't have felt a thing.

World Catcher

I am bound by net and cage
to collect. It began with small things:
a cricket and a locust;
a mussel and a crab.

Now I gather land:
a copse of trees; a ruined bridge,
its tumble of bricks spanning
one of earth's portals.

I even stow
a river or two up my sleeves,
wanting to change the course of their flow
away from the sea, towards my mouth.

This appetite will turn Elysium
into the world. No novelties;
nothing left to lose.
I am Eve, ravenous again.

Triptych

Hagtracks where we danced last night,
the coarse grass scorched
by our roundel.

Three fighting hares:
daughter, mother, mother's mother,
our doe teeth bared.

Up on our hind legs
we try to dwarf one another
but the young lusty one is tallest.

When we all leap
the moon trembles in its socket
fidgeted by our twitching,

casting its Coney eye away.
Our eldest is toughest,
she has years on her daughter,

her daughter's daughter.
She also has the sharpest temper
and her jig is hungry,

wanting the South Downs,
the poppling sea, richer pickings
than twice-widowed weeds.

We find comfort in our scrapping.
Hags or hares, our pattern
is rapture: a wreath of grass

to mark the passing of blood
between generations, the pounding
of blood in our bladed ears.

Casting

Sigils.

A rook's hooked feet.

I take my signs from rock and tree today.
They are abundant enough to restore lost faith.

Stones are washed into a round.
Cup and ring marks form spontaneously on the sand.

Joy is written, a comet, a tail that curls into a smile.
Each ellipsis has the same curve.

A rook's hooked feet.

Sigils.

Hucklebones

Find me a kissing-gate
to lean across, to reach
over for my beloved.

Pass me some hucklebones
from the knees of sheep
so I can throw and scatter them,

their pattern telling
if we shall make a pair.
I don't know yet in my gut.

Failed Medium

Miscommunication
with the spirit world
is a glass toppled
that was once in the grip
of a strong Baltic grandmother who suddenly

let go.

Vodyanoi

Who would have guessed bearded Bolsheviks
could defect to the West from their Soviet millpond?

Here they find that drowned men are neglected,
left be. Weed drips from down-turned whiskers,

lime as immature lilies, yellow as flag iris.
When the Vodyanoi crave anonymity

they assume the shape of frogs,
bellies puffed up with the assurance of peace.

If even this is not quietude enough, they lie flat,
become toppled branches, moss-covered logs,

barely sensing stagnant water
weighing like history on their haunches.

Alibini Earls of Sussex

Oules do scrike where the sweetest himnes
lately were songe,
toades and serpents hold their dennes
where the palmers did thronge.

White denizens of the churchyard,
my lords and ladies, sleep on. Oozing
ecclesiastical waters rock you, plumb
to the bottom of your opulent tombs.

Owls screech their night hymns
to mammals pinioned on the ground.
Not for your ears. Proximity to toads
need not concern you. Your sleep is sound.

Sainte Foy, Conques

Beside the Ouche, the Dourdou,
we stop at an open-air café
in the heart of the conch
opposite the abbey-church.
Here, sound comes thickly muted
(the thrown voice of confluence).
The *curieux* on the tympanum arch
– sweet-natured, crepuscular –
share their colony of agitated bats;
they swing into twilight above our heads,
liturgical utterances
from the mouths of gargoyles,
mild blasphemies
on the night's warm skin.

Saint Crispin

The patron saint of abandoned shoes,
stinging nettles and honey
were his needles and glue. *Walk on me.*

A cobbler who could fix a sole
or stitch a tongue, or fasten a sturdy eye.
Go on, kick me. Beatification has made me strong.

Abroad in Preston House, Linlithgow

Six white nymphs,
transplanted north,
support a gazebo
without expression,
silently hefting it
above their heads.

They are dwarfed
by a splendid undead yew,
its weeping bark tea-wet,
tea-red,
split
like tilled earth.

It is a gravedigger prince
giving testimony
to the lives of maids,
lamenting them
more eloquently
than an epitaph.

Is this what you'd want
when your time comes?
A single mourner
singing resin,
singing needles,
singing shade.

Two Maids

Mudmaid, Heligan

On her left side, a slice of timber
bevelled and tied to winter grass,
this maid's face is white with sleep.
Mud and moss give shape:

the contour of a clavicle; green
inner thigh. Her serene half-closed eyes
shelter more vivid woodland seeds –
a virgin's well-kept secrets.

Mermaid, Zennor

A pagan maid carved on a pew,
her frame is solid wood,
her belly-button a harvest moon
hewn from oaken skin.

She wields a cornucopia
as if it were a holy weapon.
Her scales are armoured leaves –
the chain-mail of a black icon

about to do battle with herself,
with her own dual nature.

The Exchange

The rake of the sea
is trailed by a beauty
gathering kindling stones
to fire up the moon.

Listen to the hush of it –
silver plough rustling
the small souls of sand worms
aerating the Sound.

She could be a siren
but for her two legs,
one already lame, the other
fresh with wounds.

Every sigh is hers –
raking it over,
trying to forget
bad deals made with stronger monsters.

Drifting with the Beast

I lived there
without really living,
roving its gangways like a ghost,
hardly eating, sleeping light
and feeling the chill;
fires on the beast's ship
are magically stoked,
cool green flames summoned by wishes.

Tender traces of my absent host –
a wilting flower, a grubby mirror –
were signs that he thought of me
cosmetically, Pre-Raphaelite girl in a bower.

It almost endeared him to me
but not quite enough.
The showboat of shadows
had run aground
with no-one at the tiller,
not even him.

Mock-beggar-hall

How many houses have we carved
as if they were jack-o-lanterns?
Each one a stepping-stone, a goose chase,
to find the perfect dwelling. So far
there's been no such thing, only the carriage
that rots back to pumpkin flesh at midnight,
mice swapping silver bridles for skirting-boards.

Sixteen houses in as many years.

Our fairytale: one day we'll find a lighthouse,
one to stay in, the final resting place.
She will allow the fog to swaddle her,
welcoming the sea at her concrete feet.
We tell each other she will bring our family
the kind of peace that only sleeping does –
devoid of expectation; joyless and deep.

Hey Presto!

You are on the beach again,
tide out, whispering
prestidigitation –
one of those words learned
to impress your family.

The bones of school-words – *littoral, zonal* –
lie jumbled in rock pools, casualties
of the sea's boundless self-healing,
the rearrangement of sounds.

Here, you breathe in one landscape,
breathe out another. Tide in.
Hey presto! The bones of the day
have moved, cells renewed,

and all your grey reflections
glitter again
in the strand's re-knitted marrow.

Sleight

I was in your palm
warm coin
cupped there. My security.

First I changed hands
left to right
right to left

(I was a little giddy)

then I disappeared altogether

to become a prop,
pocketed
without anyone noticing,
least of all me.

The Feel of Things

In the wake of your leaving,
I like to pleat paper,
idly fashion an impromptu fan
from the leaf of a letter.

My hand, like a child's hand,
seeks texture: the plush
of a cushion embroidered with silks,
its nap brushed backwards;

the rubber treads of a warm tyre –
elongated Zs strafing the ground
again and again – its black gullies
bas relief, hypnotic Braille.

Critical Mass

after the installation by Antony Gormley

Their nakedness is not alarming:
they are iron-cast, black as sea stone
assembled in the lustral space
where shape
and light
are part logic, part happenstance.

Beautiful at first.

After a minute or two
I want to move them,
untwist the contorted,
sit up the prone.
They look damaged, awkward,
as if there is no comfortable place.
The eye sees thrown bodies –
a battlefield scene – but that's not the story here:
they all display some voluntary pose
struck with cold deliberation.

One has his face to the white wall,
and I wonder how anyone could be content
pressed up against their shadow.

Another, head between knees,
clasps his calves, balling
into the oval of his own form.

They are all caught up in dark
adumbrations of physical grace,
this solipsistic crowd.

Still, I want to nurse them,
dress their naked self-regard,
so they are able to turn
one to another
and finally embrace.

Figure and Ground

Your upright figure,
umbrella in hand,
is softened
by snow.
You lose the matt black
gravity of a cut-out,
the stiffness,
the poker-at-the-backness,
and you begin to glow.
The oyster gestates the pearl
and what was hardboard
breaks down
in this snowmelt,
giving up
line and grain.
It's all to do with vision
of course, but all the same –
we could kiss you now.

Married on the Foreshore

I have summered and wintered you, seen the worst and best.
Is this what it means to abide? We share a laugh or two,
arm against arm, thigh against thigh. Sitting together
on the shingle, we seem a pair, a couple that holidays
companionably then retreats inland to foursquare silence.

But instead we live here amid the crunch of stones,
small leaks of brine, daily congealing of wet grey sand.
It is the habitat of lugworm, mollusc and curlew,
flat open margins refusing boundaries. In this expanse
we find desire slips through, making its oyster bed.

Sounding for the Shoals

Those blossom-white mackerel swimming on the screen –
I can't make out the lines of them; worry all is not as it should be.
At any moment they might dislodge from the ensnaring net
of sound. Their shape is so elusive I expect them to migrate,
to flock away.

My daughter's hand, arm, shoulder move – a dream of reaching,
turning. I watch her blossom in sonar; yearn for a little more focus.
Won't someone provide me with a sharper picture of her sleep?
The needle's point siphoning amniotic seas is clear. She is a cloud
nearby, indistinct.

Homunculus

Are you manikin or mandrake?
Your lips rasp
as if you haven't sipped
from the plate I put out,
but when I look
the milk has been drained.

Sorcery is new to me,
I need time to gauge
your appetites,
your waking needs.

Little man, you curl and flex
under my gaze, hands and feet
too impossibly small to grasp
this monstrous wet nurse.

At birth
your wrinkled caul was so whole
I whispered

> *perfection*
>> *perfection*

not yet afraid
of the disparities between us.

Postnatal

I never knew it would come to me
as biblical revelation, an epiphany,

so at odds with life stumbled into:
sometimes being a mother is enough.

That light inhabiting the middle-distance
was desperate to communicate;

that excited bubble of efflorescence
told me to find shelter – *a storm is coming.*

It showed me the cave.
I see it now as I close my eyes to sleep,

as I open them on a black dawn, unrefreshed,
cave cramped even though there are just us two:

me and my papoose, my small squalling bundle
of mouth and nose and ears and toes.

This is our storm – here, now – and we are safe.

Mama in the Museum of Childhood

Something of a Geisha, her black locks
hang, lacklustre serpents: pretty Medusa
like all porcelain dolls of this era.

Stone-eyed and pursed-mouthed
she chews sweet violets, nurses
the vaporous babies in specimen jars –

the Siamese piglets, the mermaid –
with contempt. There is no flesh colder
than hers. She is an unfussy mother,

the one little girls long for, neat
and so immaculately pale, bound up
in a velvet winding-sheet.

Celestial Pabulum

after the painting by Remedios Varo

Singly, I spoon stardust into
the moon-mouths of my babies,
one mouthful after another,
one baby after another,
all aligned against
the nursery wall, wailing
for a morsel, please, one more.

Don't implore me –
I will do it anyway.
Don't hurry me –
I will get to every one of you.

Drudgery is coloured
by love, of course:
what was noise, sings;
what was grey, glows.

Beyond the Moon

Through crisp winter air
Mars looks slick with the glaze of two-dimensional fruit
painted on blistered, oil-bitten canvas:

nectarine red,
separate from terrestrial colours,
made more luminous by the buff of being

hung in nothingness.
Children dream of treading lunar surfaces,
kicking white sherbet dirt, particulate and grey when it settles,

scuffing up
the pristine strands of serene seas with their footprints,
their grainy energetic marks.

But a red planet remains a firefly, a promise –
it draws the mind to the scorings, the linear pen-marks
of storytellers

who, for years, have littered its surface
with El Dorados and Erewhons.
A red planet is a rusted arrow's nib

probing beyond the moon, into the dust of us and them.

Milky Way

It is a spine,
a sinuous rope of cartilage
and bone; it casts light on you
and holds up heaven. Look,
see the animal shape of it:
a tail, a head, the familiar
shrug in the middle –
a panther hunting. Without it
that unknowable loneliness
you fear beyond measure
would come crashing down,
fragments of night
raining at your feet.

Wheal an Stearan, The Star Mine

When you glance back over your shoulder
along the mine's tin gullet,
you are surprised by distant star-shine:
one point of light in a heaven so black that,
like Orpheus, or Lot's wife,
you are humbled by the act of looking.

Tin Quartet

Coffenoola

The open-work mine of an owl
is a Wesleyan killing – a shrew
shred to its backbone, an aerial view
of small black intestines laid out.
Owl-marks litter the land, claw-
grooves and mineral-rich pellets
displayed like an Old Testament
on the lectern of Penwith.

Crease an Pocket

That crease in the kerchief
folded in half, it is deep –
a pocket of land yielding
bucket-loads of tin.

The crease of your pocket
that holds a kerchief of cloth
is shallow – mined of its stitches,
it is threadbare and thin.

Wheal Maria

Bless this bal-maiden's apron,
her white boat of a hat.
She tugs it low on her forehead
overwhelmed by heat and light.

She has worked with a miner's lust,
gradually uncovering wonders.

Wheal an Howl

In the dark there are
candles, and a bird;
six wicks: each man
has his allowance.

A small sun, an 'o',
a howl. The bird chirps
into eternity. The sun
dwindles to a silent perch.

Native Inhabitants

In a wood *(coose, cos, coys, cus, cut)*,
a stag *(carow)*;

in a mound *(creeg, creel, crig, creet)*,
the wind *(wint)*.

Siff-saff

My favourite is a summer migrant –
chiff-chaff *(siff-saff)*.
He comes in late March
to shake the catkin from the branch
with his lilt and swinging perch.

In winter, siskin *(pila gwrdd)*
play around the pond, cold
noisy raiders. They sip the seeds
dropped by old alder trees
here along the Brook of Bechan.

Bran

speaks in tongues above the battlefield,
beak like a pared stick, cocked
eye on carrion-meat.

His wings are slick black blades
with the sun on them; this day
they are staves for every felled man.

A hundred feathers, a hundred songs.
He has tumbled from heaven to stutter
his mantra again and again –

remember them, oh
           remember them,
oh –

Heronry

They are snake-necked ornaments
standing in tangled compartments,
tenemented knots that embellish the tree,
make it seem top-heavy.

Branches are upside-down gallows
hanging herons into life;
a Gordian silhouette
tars the sky

with complex nests
and scribbled birthings.

Creation of the Birds

after the painting by Remedios Varo

Owl-woman at work:
a prism and a palette,
light and colour to sculpt
a hooked claw, fine
tawny feathers. Miraculous,
this creation of the birds:
striped and mottled,
acrobat and wader;
each new child makes for
the wide-open window.

The owl-woman labours
over her desk, the plectrum
of her thumb
plucking song
into undeveloped throats.
Measured and impassive,
does she secretly hope
the wings of some won't fly,
that some will choose to wait at her side
until her job is done?

Crow Catcher

after the painting by Leonora Carrington

Once grasped, he wields the bird
as if it were an umbrella blown backwards.
Crows, rooks or ravens are what he seeks
while the air whinnies against his jowls,
rippling sallow elastic cheeks.
He wears sickle-moon skates
so he can keep up with the whirring,
shrieking corvids, each one terrified
of an incomprehensible foe.
Dervish scarecrow, his pastime isn't sport
or malice. He wants to be caught up
by the flight of scavengers and carried away
to the eye of the storm, the windless oasis.

Dog, come here into the dark house. Come here, black dog

after the etching by Leonora Carrington

Come here.
I would bring you to heel
if you weren't so tall,
towering over me with wolfish gall
and nun's tattered habit.
When I look at you
I wonder about the magic of all black dogs
resolving from mist at crossroads –
the antithesis of the Will o' the Wisp,
full of negative space, punchy dense
black matter. Your impression on the world
is one of bunching menace,
lips drawn back
over your only points of light.
But I know better: while the wind outside howls,
I can rest. You are the keeper of my dark house.

Queen of the Hedgehogs

I imagine her, all spit and spines,
brewing her own brand of vitriol
in a glass alembic. Alchemist
of the intellect, her recipe rests
upon precision, upon particulars:
proposition and refutation;
the steady accumulation of facts.

Of course, this sharpness is part
of a planned assault on knowledge,
books her ladder to esoteric heights.
But can't she dance a little,
the Queen of the Hedgehogs,
spines laid flat by moonlight,
good grog and the simple love of life?

Bickering Wife

I am a juggernaut. I have that momentum.

I am an adder; I am invisible but flick
my venom-spiked tongue at soft ankles.

I am a boulder, unable to give ground until
the shove that's strong enough to clear the way.

I am a wicker basket full to the brim
with the dead flowers of the day, words

that crisp to cinders as soon as they are out.

Cellar Spider

Your trail is in the cracks of a Belfast sink,
hairline scribbles against white porcelain.

Here, in this house, you are Victorian graffiti
of a kind that rarely interrupts the day –

people can work around you; I work around you
eyeing your Penny Black back, your febrile lines

shivering in the sudden draft as I pass.
Like me, you are so British: mildly venomous

if provoked, suspended between two points
without even a nod to contingency.

Purse-web Spider

Up close, your grape-body is bulbous,
semi-opaque. All belly.
You fit in the snug of a lady's glove,
thick silk, a probing fingerful.

Bits and bones aren't held in the crook
for long: they are spat out, neatly picked,
glove fabric mended
almost as soon as it tears.

You never choose what to wear or eat.
Your life has little glamour, few wants –
you are lost in your frugal feasts,
the dense fur of your knitted lair.

It must be easy to dwell
in a self-healing funnel,
small stowaway at the ball,
sensing opportunities and seizing them.

Anatomy of the Spider

I admire your book lungs:
pale squares on the underside
of your abdomen.
What a way to breathe! –
through the open flicking
of pages, carousel of words,
each passing inhalation
a meal of paper and air,
a tiny education.

Silks

To have both trapeze and anchor,
a spinning umbilical sheet
to shinny up and down,
Rapunzel-style, is what somnambulists dream of:

your dragline. It swings in the breeze,
becomes meadow-hair at dawn,
multiplies. When gossamer catches first light
night-walkers have the path back to their beds.

*

Silk from your spinnerets
is drawn by leg, like milk by hand
or sweet floss that folds into shape
on the stick: a long shaggy tale
of flight and captivity,
goddesses and weavers;
hidden stories hardening
under the light. It is not ectoplasm
or effluvium. Nothing is wasted.

It is a template, a blueprint,
this proto-silk,
an aeronaut's chute
that opens at the last minute
to take shape on the wind.

On the Road from Men-an-Tol

A wayside sacrifice:
a pumpkin, flowers, a quince.

I kneel beside them,
touch their stems and skins,

warm and aromatic as fresh tarmac.
I wonder who left them

plucked ripe for the gifting
without any expectation of return.

The quince affects me most:
apple of Venus, golden coin;

its unripe rind, like yellow furze,
prickles my fingers when I lift it

from the ground. It is meant
to percolate in rosewater, musk,

flavouring a slow-cooked compote.
Otherwise inedible. I'll keep it,

watch it rot back to strings of seeds
in the sun and rain on my northern sill,

until all that remains of the fruit I was given
is bitter juice, spilling into soil.

Pot Roast

On a Cretan hill in winter
the stench of lamb on a spit
is an ancestral offering;
oily blue mountain smoke
wreathes my neck, I gag –
reflex like a backwards glance.

A cat slinks up to leftovers,
belly slack from many litters.
Somehow, I can see inside
her head – deposed icon,
old totem starved of deity.
She is just one more drifting
mote in the evening's pot roast,
one more charred grey particle.

The road I was following is lost now,
swallowed whole by hungry ghosts.

Sheep's Skull and Weir

When we walked the length of Lathkill Dale
on the day of the dead sheep, you pointed out
a pair of dippers, crazy birds, romancing the river
like oversized insects. I envied their rollercoaster.
Downstream we saw it, shanks shored up in mud,
separated skull caught bleached and bobbing
at the foot of a weir. *You could write a poem about it.*
Its Orphic sockets watched, almost daring me.
But nothing came then. No prophetic couplets
issued from the upturned knuckly cranium,
no fragments of divided flesh swam together
to knit a living creature. All it said to me was,
Miracles are rare. I would love to prove it wrong.

Old Shore More

Reaching Old Shore More
is finding one golden egg
among brown dozens.

Mainland beach, its yolk
an island in albumen.
Worries are shed here

near Scotland's north tip,
bitterness a pebble skimmed
into the blue Minch.

Eleven Islands

Eleven islands
seen from Cullipool,
though I'm not sure
if some are islands
or just rocks,
or if I can remember
their proper names,
though one must be
the Ross of Mull,
and I know one is flat
and one is long
in the Norseman's blunt
settler-tongue.

Marram

The smallest dune, knee-bent,
almost a Canute
before the winter sea,

has hair like wire.
It would split your webbing
if you ran your fingers through it,

leaving black blood in the gold
and fine white scars
upon your hands.

See its cross-hatching, its barbed
shape hunched against
the wind. A last defence.

You could learn from it,
how to turn your back
on spit and foam.

You come here, an alien,
far away from home,
crouched in dunes

as if they weren't rough beacons,
or hostile bastions,
or outposts.

A Quiet Word

You know the wind howls
but you can't hear it.

You are taciturn,
failing to love the world you're in,
its elements.

Your ears are blocked with rags
and a visor shields your eyes.

I often see you dressed like that
when you start on the garden,
opening the shed for your tools.

By evening, you have unravelled
slightly, rags flapping,

and you dig to the rhythm of the sea.
Let it go, I say, let it all go.
But I say it silently.

Hiatus

A strip of paper snapping
in the wind, white pennant
pointing compass directions.
Sometimes it gutters and stops,
letting go like a prayer-wheel at rest;
no prayers flying to the gods above,
to the four corners.
It is pretty science,
this white page
with its invisible ink and lemon juice
left to hang out and dry
in the new warm southerly
summoned under suspended breath.

Delabole Wind Farm

When I was an aeronaut
with a flapping scarf and
oversized Biggles goggles
I flew an oddball's plane:

a turbine of three blades
atop a high mast, straining
in the viper winds that whipped
straight off the Atlantic.

As I ogled the compass
and adjusted my course,
I would ponder the price
of this aeronautical life –

loneliness, the loss
of a sense of groundedness.
But electricity never failed
to thump the sky back into my heart.

Narcís Monturiol

The sub's engines thrum
a grey and morbid beat
until a bubble-man appears on deck
to entertain the crowds:

with a skein of wire
to dip in buckets of suds,
he creates a warped
and trembling behemoth

of light and air and water in balance.

This man's vision
nimbly blown through the hoop
is so big that all clouds disperse
before a thousand skerries of colour.

They ask him, is he Nemo or Charon?
Neither, he says, *listen only to this*:

From today, all men are brothers,
there will be no slave or master.

Let us march, march onward, Icarians,
holding up the banner of love.

But to live within his tenuous walls
is impossible.

So far from the docks of Barcelona,
the sun and optimism of Catalonia,
perhaps he realises the size of the feat.
His protean world of light and air and water in balance

deliquesces and flicks off like a thrown switch.

Flat Raft

Pulled across the Adur
one swallocky day
on a flat raft, cows

were restless,
mother's long skirts curled
against her wet legs,

and all the children sat
at the end nearest
the animal reek,

elders up-wind.
It was a squashed day when
mud was water, water mud

and blood ran slowly in the veins.
All the talk and noise couldn't
blot the buzz of the river

swollen with summer,
dying of it, from one boy.
He held the tiller of a modern

ship in his hand, sailed into
another age, just from wishing
the air be a mite thinner.

Static

A single caravan in a field of cropped corn
has a sagging awning to give just
one small square of shade. Not enough.

Washing wrinkles on the line, dry in an eye-blink.
A boy squints at it: black tropic
on an invisible globe of heat. He is a lizard

who barely breathes on the metal step.
His plastic soldiers have all been sacrificed,
sweating out action poses until their little deaths.

Cicadas

Sometimes called jar flies,
you remember them best
as dry flies – the summer swarm
in DC a kind of half-death,
only simulacra left in their wake:
small mouthparts, perfect wings.

You could trade them
with your friends, make a line
of cicada infantrymen,
cupping their husks
inside hot plump palms.
The part that was a nymph
preserved; the other
older part
squirming out of its mould,
reborn from humidity.

Dog days were leavened
by the lifecycle of the cicada –
insects ageing, shedding,
gone, zeds in their ticking.
You dreamed of more exotic cities
littered with bodies, sizzling with song.

Freak Phenomena

Siphoned from their beds,
periwinkles crack open
on Beijing pavements;

storm-addled tadpoles
carpet downtown Kolkata;
red ants rain on Bonn.

Loose tongues spread the news:
the Second Coming, world's end!
But what harbingers –

tiny, untarnished.

Groom

He is used to mucking them out,
licking oat-flecks from their eyes,
calming them. Odin's steeds
bear bad weather on their backs.

He is the groom who takes their reins
in his pale hands, leads them
to the sky's pink and pulsing heart,
to their stentorian master.

Every day, he wakes up
to the pewter stable-stink
of new stormed earth,
wishing to be born again in peace.

Port-boys

The port-boys are massing,
sign of consternation. Should I stay
or wander away like weather?

So much is enshrined in the backbone
of hills that stretches along the coast:
all those years cradled against the belly

of the sea. But the wind is calling me north
to follow my vanished father's path,
as if he were a river and I were charged

with opening up its source.

West Pier, Brighton

Rollercoaster
into the sea,
I love to look at
your vagrancy
and let my thoughts migrate
to other phantoms:

the collapsed body of a sunken skiff,
knuckles dragged along the seabed;

the dogs-clouds that appear in mist,
dissolve in mist, bemusing fishermen;

my own reflection, cast like a line
into the dark waves, leaning

over the end of the pier that disappeared.

Painting the Lines

in memoriam Jo

Tension radiates from the skull,
the crown of the hill, ley lines
incised in white chalk. Distance
softens them to froth, but up close
they are hard, they bite
into the shallow topsoil of the Downs,
making their marks in spite of resistance.

People think of ley lines, old ways,
as finite things, paths to be followed,
fates to be met. You painted them,
skein of geese flying over the green,
webs criss-crossing a tilled field with
tapering silks; the end of the track
always absent, beyond your frame.

Hat of Heaven

If I were a hatter,
I would take a length of silk ribbon
and work in comets –
ill-omened tails stretching out
beyond the coattails of the wearer.

To offset superstition I would weave in
other optical effects that augur health –
a sundog, a double rainbow.
It would be a hat of heaven, all vaults and air,
the ribbon buffeted like a topsail

about a wicker frame.
This basket of winds would bring my client
vigour and clarity: the ability to always see
beyond the atmosphere
to a brace of vagrant stars.

De Natura Rerum

Far away, forked lightning over the sea
scores cloud bellies with skeletal fingers.
Clear, tree-like, it is an after-image
made small by a long twenty-five miles, tinged
pink by the dwindling sun. And so remote
it makes me lonely, makes me long for it:
someone else's fortune, some ill-starred boat,
scorched. Not mine. Tonight the Channel stays lit
until all power is sourced, all sea is earthed.
I linger here on Worthing's shingle edge
witnessing storm's end, its natural still-birth,
palms finally unclasping, nail-mark red.
Then walk inland, excitement discharging.
Never the centre, always the margin.

When the Sun Turns Green

A green line on the horizon –
not marsh gas, not camera flash,
not the northern lights.
A last gasp, a pea-soup haze,
the cambered ray as the sun dips
into dust. Don't look away –
it is quick, a quick green life.

Notes

Vodyanoi
In Russia, the Vodyanoi ('umber hulk') are mythical creatures
inhabiting the bottom of deep bodies of fresh water.

Alibini Earls of Sussex
The Alibini (or D'Aubigny) Earls have tombs in Arundel Cathedral.
The text in italics is an extract from 'A Lament for Our Lady's Shrine at
Walsingham', an Elizabethan ballad written to mourn the loss of a
place of pilgrimage. Traditionally, it has been ascribed to Philip
Howard, but the authorship remains uncertain.

Critical Mass
Critical Mass by sculptor Antony Gormley consists of sixty solid cast-
iron body-forms in a variety of poses.

Mock-beggar-hall
Mock-beggar-hall (Sussex dialect): a house which has an inviting
external aspect, but within is poor and bare, dirty and disappointing.
(*A Dictionary of the Sussex Dialect by the Reverend W. D. Parish*,
reprinted by Snake River Press, 2008)

Native Inhabitants
The italicised words are in Cornish.

Siff-saff
The italicised words are in Welsh.

Bran
Bran (Welsh): raven. The Celtic goddess Morrighan was often thought
to be present at battles in the form of a raven.

Narcís Monturiol
The lines in italics are the lyrics to the anthem of the socialist and
utopist group the Icarians, founded in 1847 in Barcelona. Printer and

editor of the communist newspaper *La Fraternidad*, Narcís Monturiol also established the first commercial society in Spain dedicated to the exploration of submarine navigation.

Port-boys

Port-boys are small low clouds in a clear sky.

JANE McKIE, originally from West Sussex, lives in Linlithgow, West Lothian. Her poems have been published in various magazines and anthologies, including *New Writing Scotland* and Granta's *New Writing* Volume 15. Her first collection, *Morocco Rococo* (Cinnamon Press), was awarded the Sundial/Scottish Arts Council prize for best first book of 2007. She runs a small press, Knucker Press (www.knuckerpress.com), which brings together writers and artists in books and pamphlets in a way that is mutually illustrative and fulfilling. With the support of the Scottish Arts Council, Jane is beginning work on a third collection in 2009.